CHRONOS CRIME CHRONICLES

Jane Parker:

The Downfall of Two Tudor Queens?

JOHN HUNT PUBLISHING

First published by Chronos Books, 2021
Chronos Books is an imprint of John Hunt Publishing Ltd., No. 3 East St., Alresford,
Hampshire SO24 9EE, UK
office@jhpbooks.com
www.johnhuntpublishing.com
www.chronosbooks.com

For distributor details and how to order please visit the 'Ordering' section on our website.

ISBN: 978 1 78904 443 0
978 1 78904 444 7 (ebook)
Library of Congress Control Number: 2020934426

A CIP catalogue record for this book is available from the British Library.

Design: Stuart Davies

UK: Printed and bound by CPI Group (UK) Ltd, Croydon, CR0 4YY
Printed in North America by CPI GPS partners

We operate a distinctive and ethical publishing philosophy in
all areas of our business, from our global network of authors to
production and worldwide distribution.

Contents

To my parents, who have supported me throughout my research and indulged my love of history, putting up with many trips to castles and historic sites.

Introduction

'For this principal matter between the queen and her brother, there was brought forth, indeed, witness, his wicked wife accuser of her own husband, even to the seeking of his blood, which I believe is hardly to be showed of any honest woman ever done. But of her, the judgement that fell out upon her, and the just punishment by law after of her naughtiness, show that what she did was more to be rid of him than of true ground against him.'[1]

These are the words George Wyatt used to describe Jane Parker, Lady Rochford, near the end of Elizabeth I's reign. Wyatt accused Jane of plotting against her husband and sister-in-law, Anne Boleyn, and stated that she deserved her downfall alongside another Tudor queen, Katherine Howard. This has also been the general consensus among recent historians, with Eric Ives calling Jane 'Anne's enemy' and Lacey Baldwin-Smith going so far as to call her a 'pathological meddler, with most of the instincts of a procuress who achieves a vicarious pleasure from arranging assignations'.[2] However, no contemporary account described her as such and the sources used by these historians are of a later date, when they had the benefit of hindsight and knew she was executed for being involved in Katherine Howard's affair with Thomas Culpepper.

Jane Parker was the wife of George Boleyn and served five of Henry VIII's six wives, but has remained mainly in the shadows until now. When she has been mentioned in the past, it has been in connection with either Anne Boleyn or Katherine Howard, not as her own person, and any mention of her has almost always been a negative one. Her portrayals in the popular TV series *The Tudors* and *Wolf Hall* has not helped matters, with them depicting her as the spiteful wife who willingly approached Thomas Cromwell with evidence against her husband and Anne Boleyn, and, in the case of *The Tudors*, even as a voyeur to Katherine Howard and Culpepper's passionate relationship.

Jane's involvement with Katherine and her own downfall alongside her has coloured our view of her and many have failed to take into account the difficult position she was in and the intense mental strain she was under, which resulted in a nervous breakdown while in custody. She may have helped Katherine meet Culpepper, but she likely had no choice in the matter and was not the willing participant she has often been made out to be.

This book will seek to tell the true story of Jane Parker, dispelling the myths and looking at her as a woman who was just trying to survive in the dangerous world of the Tudor court. It aims to present a faithful view of her marriage to George, that of a convenient but not unhappy relationship, something that is rarely seen in other books on the subject. Jane will be history's scapegoat for no longer.

Chapter 1

Early Life

Jane Parker was the daughter of Henry Parker, Lord Morley, and his wife, Alice St John. She was one of at least four children the couple had after their marriage sometime between 1499 and 1503, although only three of the children achieved much of significance to add to the historical record. She would have lived a comfortable life as the daughter of one of the lords of the land.[1] Morley had served in Margaret Beaufort's household when he was younger and so his loyalty was firmly established and, with the Wars of the Roses over, Jane could expect a fairly secure and even happy future.

As with the majority of Tudor women, we do not have a precise date of birth for Jane and so we have to make an estimate using the evidence we have available. One of the most valuable pieces of evidence is the skeleton that was suggested to be Jane herself, unearthed in the nineteenth century. After doing some work on the floor of the chapel of St. Peter ad Vincula in the Tower of London, the skeletons of those interred there were examined and documented. After finding no skeleton in the place where Katherine Howard was said to have been buried, it was reported that:

'The portions of the skeleton of the second female found, were those of a woman probably of forty years of age, of larger frame than Katharine Howard. They may possibly therefore have been those of Lady Rochford, who was executed at the same time.'[2]

This would, therefore, place Jane at around the same age as that of her future husband, George Boleyn, whose birth date has been suggested as being between 1503 and 1504, with 1504 being the more likely of the two.[3] There was no mention of a notable age gap between the two either when the marriage was being arranged or after and, had there been one, those like George Wyatt who wrote against her years later surely would have used it to support their theory of her being a jealous woman and in an unhappy marriage. We can say with as much certainty as possible with the scant evidence we have available that Jane was born around 1504 or 1505.

Jane grew up in the manor of Great Hallingbury in Essex, the Morley family seat. It had descended with the title through the Lovell family to the Parkers, in which the barony was revived.[4]

Having been born into a wealthy and well-connected family, her parents would have soon started planning for her future. Several years after her birth, a new king had come to the throne, bringing with him hope for a happier England after the paranoia and numerous taxes under Henry VII. Henry VIII's reign also brought hope of a livelier court, as his wife, the Spanish Katherine of Aragon, was the first queen consort since Elizabeth of York's death six years ago. Managing to secure a place for their daughter at this court would have been one of the highest honours for the Parkers, it would ensure she made valuable connections and she might even meet her future husband there.

England was a Catholic country at the time of Jane's birth and so she would have been raised as such. Her father, Lord Morley, was a staunch Catholic himself and would continue to be one even after Henry VIII's break with Rome, having a good relationship with Princess Mary but still managing to stay in the king's good books.

We do not know much about Jane's early life, but we know that, sometime in early 1520, Morley managed to secure his daughter a place at court, serving Queen Katherine of Aragon as a maid of honour. A position at court was a privilege and one that many young women would have aspired to, it was a way of representing and furthering their family as well as having the ear of the queen. Jane would have been around 16 or 17 years old at the time, an age at which she would also have been anticipating a match being made for her, and would have no idea just where this path would lead her.

Chapter 2

At Henry VIII's Court

We know that Jane arrived at court in time to see the spectacular event that was the Field of Cloth of Gold, as a 'mistres Parker' is recorded in the Calais Chronicle as having attended, alongside another notable woman, 'mistres Carie'.[1] Mistress Carey was Mary Boleyn, Jane's future sister-in-law and a woman who would soon become one of Henry VIII's mistresses. The Field of Cloth of Gold was a celebration of the treaty between Henry VIII and Francis I of France, which had been made in 1514, and there was some hope that it would increase the friendship between the two kings. It was held in June 1520, so we know that Jane had at least entered service sometime before the event. She may not have even had the chance to settle into court life, with the Field of Cloth of Gold being one of the first and most notable experiences of her career.

As a maid of honour, Jane would have served the Queen with other unmarried ladies and they would have been expected to polish their manners and learn useful skills that would make them a good wife to a well-born gentleman. Despite the honour of having the ear of the Queen, the tasks Jane would have been required to perform could be quite menial at times. Outside of court events, such as the Field of Cloth of Gold, she could have been called on to hold a basin of water for the Queen to wash her hands in before dinner or hold a cloth before her face for her to spit into.[2]

However, there were some other benefits to being a maid of honour. Jane would have been given free accommodation and permitted one servant and a spaniel.[3] Each maid was entitled to a breakfast of a chine of beef, two loaves of bread and a gallon of ale, with similar portions for the remaining meals. They were also paid annual salaries, which rose from £5 to £10 during Henry VIII's reign, so from £2,600 to £4,213 in today's money.[4]

The court events would have been one of the highlights of the position. Jane participated in several of these, including another one with her future sister-in-law, Mary Boleyn. In 1522, Jane was one of those starring in the Chateau Vert. Hall's Chronicle records that there were several court ladies dressed as different virtues:

> 'this castle was kept with ladies of straunge names, the first Beautie, the second Honor, the third Perseueraunce, the fourth Kyndnes, the fifth Constance, the sixte Bountie, the seuenthe Mercie, and the eight Pitie'[5]

Jane played the virtue Constancy and Mary played Kindness.[6] This event was notable as it also included Jane's other future sister-in-law, Anne Boleyn, who played Perseverance in the pageant. Anne had only recently returned to England after having served at the court of Margaret of Austria since she was a young girl. She would have known French and how to dance and make music, making her appearance at the English court noteworthy and enough to draw attention from the people there and perhaps even envy from the other women, who might have felt upstaged by this new arrival.

We do not know how Jane felt about Anne, but she would soon become closer to her than she could have ever expected. It was not long after this event that Jane's father started making arrangements for a suitable marriage for her. The man was someone she would have known from her time at court, George Boleyn.

Chapter 3

Marriage

Jane was now of an age to enter the marriage market and soon a marriage was arranged which would join the Parkers with one of the rising stars of court, George Boleyn. His family were highly in favour during the 1520s and so this was an advantageous match that Morley made for his daughter. Jane would have known her proposed groom as they had both been at court together. She may not have known him well but this was more than most women could expect, and, if we accept that Jane was born around 1505 and George in 1504, they were a similar age when they married and so in a better position than many arranged marriages at the time.

Jane's marriage to George Boleyn was one of several marriages cementing an alliance between the Parkers and the Boleyns. Jane's sister, Margaret Parker, married Sir John Shelton, whose mother was the sister of Anne Boleyn's father. This would be useful as the Boleyns were rising fast at court, although how far they would rise none could guess.

We have no official date for when Jane and George married, however, we can estimate that it was sometime between late 1524 and early 1525. We know they were married by January 1526 because, as historian Julia Fox discovered when using ultraviolet light, Wolsey mentioned George's wife in a grant given to him at the time. Wolsey writes that he was to have 'twenty pounds yearly above the eighty pounds he hath gotten to him and his wife to live thereupon'.[1] Jane's jointure, which was an amount paid to her if she survived her husband, was signed on 4 October 1524 and so the wedding would have taken place not long after that and sometime before January 1526, when Wolsey mentioned the couple.[2]

The majority of historians state that Jane and George had an unhappy marriage, however no contemporary reports say this. There is little to no mention of their marriage in any account and this leads us to the conclusion that there was nothing out of the ordinary about their relationship. They may not have had any children, but George was often away from court on diplomatic missions abroad and, besides being physically apart from each other, they might just have not been capable of having children.

Other than the fact that they had no children, some importance has been placed on a book George owned on marriage. George was once in possession of a French translation of a Latin poem entitled Les Lamentations de Matheolus, which is a satirical work on women and marriage. On one of the first pages, he makes it clear that it is his work, writing 'thys boke ys myn George Boleyn 1526'.[3] Retha Warnicke takes the date of his signature as being significant, as it is around the time it is estimated that George and Jane married, suggesting that the fact that the author of the book 'lamented the great sadness of his soul and dated the beginning of all his torments from the day he was wed' supports the idea that it was an unhappy marriage.[4] However, this book had several owners and seems to have been passed around a certain group of people at court, comprising of both unmarried and married men. This includes Thomas Wyatt, who admittedly did have an unhappy marriage, but also Mark Smeaton, who was unmarried, and who wrote in the book as well.[5] What is often overlooked is the fact that this book also includes Jehan le Fevre's refutation of Les Lamentations, making it a more balanced account of marriage than it initially seems at first glance.

Warnicke uses the fact that George gave this book to Mark Smeaton to support her theory as to George's homosexuality, one that has been widely discredited, and suggests that this was another reason why George's marriage to Jane was unhappy.[6] However, Warnicke is one of the only people who believes this theory and the latest research into George's life has shown that the myth of his homosexuality is down to a misinterpretation of certain sources, like his execution speech, and so cannot be used as evidence for an unhappy marriage.[7]

Retha Warnicke has placed great importance on George Cavendish's Metrical Visions poem as evidence for George's homosexuality and unhappy marriage with Jane. In Cavendish's work, he talks about his womanising and tells the reader that:

> *'My lyfe not chastt / my lyvyng bestyall*
> *I fforced wydowes / maydens I did deflower*
> *All was oon to me / I spared non at all*
> *My appetit was / all women [to] devoure'*[8]

Warnicke takes Cavendish's description of George's living as being 'bestyall' as evidence of his homosexuality, however that is directly contradicted by the following lines, where he is described as a rapist and womaniser. Either way, this does not paint a good view of his marriage to Jane as, even though there is no direct mention of her, it shows he is not against forcing women and seeking solace elsewhere. However, we have to take this with a pinch of salt. Cavendish had a grudge against the Boleyns, especially as they were, either directly or indirectly, responsible for the downfall of his former master, Cardinal Wolsey. As no one else mentions this side of George Boleyn, we can dismiss this as an attack against a member of the family he hated.

Chapter 4

Serving Anne Boleyn

Shortly after Jane and George married, the world as they knew it started to change. Henry VIII's ever-wandering eye had turned on Anne, Jane's sister-in-law, and he was determined to make her his wife. This would have made things difficult for Jane, seeing as she had originally been sent to court to serve Queen Katherine of Aragon, yet now there was the prospect of Katherine being replaced as queen by a Boleyn, a family Jane was now very much a part of. However, despite it being awkward in the interim, there was still the prospect of being related to one of the most powerful people in the country, something that neither Jane nor her family could have possibly imagined when they arranged her marriage to George.

However, all looked like it might come to nothing for, in 1528, disaster struck. Both Anne and George came down with the Sweating Sickness. We do not know exactly what it was but it recurred several times throughout this period. Jane was probably with George and the court at the time, as Anne only left to go to Hever Castle after one of her maids fell ill. Anne became sick in June and Henry quickly sent a physician to her.[1] We know that Jane's husband also became ill sometime in 1528 as, in an undated letter to Anne, the King wrote that he fell ill while they were at Waltham. However, he then says that he was now well again, so it seems that he recovered quickly:

'When we were at Waltham, two ushers, two valuts de chambre, your brother, master "Jesonere" (Treasurer), fell ill, and are now quite well; and we have since removed to Hunsden, where we are very well, without one sick person.'[2]

It sounds like Anne only heard of George's illness sometime after he had recovered. This was sometime around June of that year, as Brian Tuke comments on the recovery of both Anne and George in a letter to Cardinal Wolsey on 22 June:

> 'how Mistress Ann (Boleyn) and my lord Rochford both have had it; what jeopardy they have been in by the turning in of the sweat before the time; of the endeavor of Mr. Buttes, who hath been with them in his return; and finally of their perfect recovery.'[3]

There is no mention of Jane, which may have been because she was not as important as Anne and George, however it seems strange that Henry would not have mentioned her in the letter to Anne if she had become ill. It, therefore, stands to reason that she was one of the lucky ones who did not catch the Sweating Sickness.

There was more good news later that year, as George took on his father's title of Viscount Rochford on 8 December 1529, after Thomas Boleyn was made the Earl of Wiltshire. It was initially a courtesy title but it became his officially in 1533 when he became a peer in his own right. This meant that Jane was now called Lady Rochford, a title that she would continue to use after her husband's death.

Jane accompanied her husband when they went to France for the meeting between Henry VIII and Francis I in October 1532, where Henry hoped to gain Francis' approval for his marriage to Anne Boleyn.[4] This would have been one of the few times she was able to travel with her husband and perhaps even spend some time with him. Once they arrived in Calais, Jane would have been one of the seven masked ladies who danced for the French king, something that may have reminded her of the Field of Cloth of Gold. Much had changed for Jane since that event, one of the first of her career at court.

Around this time, Anne finally allowed the King to come to

her bed. Jane would have been one of the first to know, being her sister-in-law and undoubtedly one of her closest ladies. It would not be long before she fell pregnant and matters had to be resolved quickly in order to ensure the legitimacy of her child. We cannot be sure as to whether Jane was at the secret wedding of Henry and Anne, but she would have at least known about it.

Events moved at a fast pace in 1533, with Henry VIII's marriage to Katherine of Aragon being annulled on 23 May 1533 and the marriage between Henry and Anne Boleyn declared valid on 29 May, leading to Anne's coronation at Westminster Abbey on 1 June. Jane would have been with Anne every step of the way and must have been just as excited as she, although perhaps feeling some pity for the queen she had served previously.

We do not have it, but we know Jane sent a letter to her husband in regards to the coronation proceedings, as referenced in a letter Sir Edward Baynton wrote to George in June 1533.[5] This was one of the most important moments in their lives and, despite being separated, they were both very much involved in the various aspects of Anne's coronation and procession.

Just over a month before Anne's coronation, on 29 April 1533, Jane's husband was rewarded for his loyalty to the king and his cause and was granted the wardship of Edmund Sheffield.[6] He was the son of Sir Robert Sheffield and was a distant relative of the king, as well as the heir to lands in Nottinghamshire and Lincolnshire. This wardship would have brought in significant income for George and Jane, mainly through the administration of his inheritance, and was one of the many rewards they received for their service and close relationship with the king.

Jane and George were riding high, with Jane at some point even supporting a scholar at King's College, Cambridge, a man called William Foster. A few years later, he would call her the 'most special patronness of my stody [study]' and this suggests she may have either financed or at least subsided him.[7] This reveals a lot about Jane's character and interest in education, an interest probably instilled in her by her father, a well-known translator of books, as well as showing us how secure she must have been financially to be able to support this scholar.[8]

On 26 August 1533, Anne Boleyn went into confinement for the birth of her child, the future Elizabeth I.[9] This was the usual ritual for women of high status, in which they would be kept in a chamber for four to six weeks before the birth and surrounded only by their ladies, which, for Anne, would have included Jane. Anne may have miscalculated or Elizabeth may have been born premature, as she gave birth two weeks later. On 7 September, Elizabeth was born and Jane became an aunt. She may not have been the longed-for prince but there was still reason to be hopeful, as she was born healthy and with no complications. There was every reason to hope that a son would soon follow.

Anne fell pregnant again in 1534, as Eustace Chapuys reported on 28 January that she 'is now pregnant and in condition to have more children'.[10] Historians are still unsure as to what exactly happened with this pregnancy, as at one time Jane's husband was being sent to France to ask for the postponement of a meeting between Henry VIII and Francis I because of Anne's condition, and then we hear nothing more.[11] Anne is likely to have either had a miscarriage or a phantom pregnancy, which would have been a devastating blow for both her and the whole Boleyn family, including Jane. It seemed that history may have been repeating itself, with Anne having fallen under the same curse as Katherine of Aragon, and would have been a stark reminder of Jane's own apparent failure in bearing her husband a child to carry on the Boleyn name.

Anne likely would have confided in Jane and may have done so in the aftermath of her miscarriage. One notable instance of Anne doing so was later that same year, in October 1534. In one of Eustace Chapuys' despatches to Charles V, he writes that Jane 'has been banished the Court because she had conspired with the... Concubine to procure the withdrawal from Court of the young lady whom this king has been accustomed to serve'.[12] Anne and Jane had hatched a scheme, we are not told what it consisted of, to have Henry's latest mistress removed from the court. This failed and Jane was banished instead, but it shows Jane's loyalty to the Boleyn cause and there is no word of any bad feeling between the two when she returned.

We have little information on Jane as it is and any trace of her goes cold during her banishment from court. She may have stayed at the Palace of Beaulieu, which had been granted to her husband by the King and would certainly have been a comfortable place to keep her head down and wait to be allowed to return.

Returning from court after her banishment a few months later, Jane must have hoped that things would get back to normal. There was a new royal baby on the way, Henry had lost interest in his mistress, and everything was looking more positive. However, what she couldn't anticipate was that her life would soon change forever.

Chapter 5

The Downfall of Anne and George Boleyn

It is hard to pinpoint exactly when Jane returned to court after her banishment. Julia Fox suggests that she returned sometime in early 1535, just before the executions of John Fisher and Thomas More, and around the time Henry VIII lost interest in the mistress who had caused so much trouble.[1] This seems plausible as it would have been a time where the King would have been distracted with other matters and the incident with Jane would have seemed far less important.

Just because Jane had been banished before, does not mean she now decided to stay in the shadows and keep to herself. One instance which has thrown some doubt on Jane's relationship with her sister-in-law is when Jane joined a crowd who were protesting against the harsh treatment of Henry VIII's eldest daughter, the Lady Mary, in 1535. The Bishop of Tarbes wrote in a letter to the Bailly of Troyes in October of that year that:

> 'when she [Mary] was removed from Greenwich, a great troop of citizens' wives and others, unknown to their husbands, presented themselves before her, weeping and crying that she was Princess, notwithstanding all that had been done. Some of them, the chiefest, were placed in the Tower, constantly persisting in their opinion.'[2]

At first glance, this seems to be of little importance to the story of Jane Parker, however, in the margin of the letter there is a note which states 'Millor de Rochesfort et millord de Guillaume'.[3] 'Millor de Rochesfort' is referring to George Boleyn, Lord Rochford, and so we can infer from this reference that Jane Parker was one of the wives who were involved in the protest in favour of the Lady Mary.[4] However, there is no evidence that she was one of those arrested and taken to the Tower of London. If Jane was involved in an incident like this it certainly would have been mentioned, with her being the sister-in-law of the Queen. Many other Boleyn supporters were against the way Mary had been treated, so it was not unusual for her to be too and does not mean she was any less loyal to her new family's cause. Jane did, in fact, stay in close contact with Mary, even more so after the Boleyns' fall and Mary's return to favour, as there is a record of numerous gifts passing between the two from 1536 to 1538.[5] It has been suggested that this was the reason for her apparent betrayal of the Boleyns and that her family, her father, Lord Morley, in particular, had long been close to Mary, but this has been discounted by David Starkey, who called it 'absurd' and said that this 'supposed loyalty rather begs the question of why Morley had sought a double marriage alliance with the Boleyns'.[6] We do not in fact know if or how this had an impact on Jane's relationship with Anne, but there was no break in her time at court, other than the temporary banishment that was mentioned earlier, and she continued to serve Anne until her arrest in May 1536, with no mention of any discord between the two women. Since an intimate discussion with Anne about Henry VIII's sexual problems came after this event, we can reliably say that the relationship between Jane and Anne did not suffer from any support Jane gave Mary.

As 1536 approached, the future initially looked bright. There was a new royal baby on the way, as Anne was pregnant again, and the couple seemed fairly secure in their affections for each other. However, no one could have predicted how drastically the fortunes of the Boleyn family would change in that year, least of all Jane. The first sign that the year was going to be a bad one was the loss of Henry and Anne's longed-for son on 29 January 1536, ironically on the day of Katherine of Aragon's funeral. The Spanish Ambassador, Eustace Chapuys wrote that:

'On the same day that the Queen [Katherine of Aragon] was buried this King's concubine miscarried of a child, who had the appearance of a nude about three months and a half old, at which miscarriage the King has certainly shown great disappointment and sorrow... Upon the whole, the general opinion is that the concubine's miscarriage was entirely owing to defective constitution, and her utter inability to bear male children; whilst others imagine that the fear of the King treating her as he treated his late Queen, - which is not unlikely, considering his behaviour towards a damsel of the Court, named Miss Seymour, to whom he has latterly made very valuable presents – is the oral cause of it all.'[7]

To see her mistress so distressed would have been difficult for Jane, even more so as everyone knew that by then Henry's eye had been turned by Jane Seymour, another one of the women who served Anne. There was a fear that she would now be discarded in favour of his latest mistress and, emotional attachment to her sister-in-law aside, where would that leave Jane Parker? Despite some lingering sympathy for the Lady Mary, she was a member of the Boleyn family now and could well end up on the losing side if Anne did not win the King back.

On 2 May 1536, Anne Boleyn was arrested and taken to the Tower of London, soon to be followed by her husband George and several other men. There are many myths surrounding Jane and her involvement, or, in reality, lack of involvement, in the downfall of Anne and George Boleyn. The most popular allegation made against Jane is that she accused Anne and George of committing incest, which needs to be explored in detail.

There are several references to Jane Parker throughout May 1536, however, none of them mentions her accusing Anne Boleyn, if anything they paint her in a more positive light. During George Boleyn's imprisonment, Jane is recorded by Sir William Kingston as having sent a message to her husband in the Tower of London. Even though his reports were damaged in a fire in 1731, we can still read enough to know that she was doing what she could for him and was going to try to intercede with the king on his behalf, as 'she wold humly sut unto the kynges hy[nes[... for her husband'.[8] We have no record of her attempt, but this does not mean she did not try and, if she was working for Cromwell to bring about the downfall of her husband, there would have been no reason to send a letter to him making false promises.

Diarmaid MacCulloch, in his new biography on Thomas Cromwell, confidently asserts that the fact that Lord Morley, Jane's father, was granted the stewardship of Hatfield Park after the Boleyns fall, which had previously been held by his late son-in-law, shows that the family was being rewarded for Jane's part in the events of 1536.[9] However, this is a stretch by anyone's standards, as the spoils of the Boleyns' fall were being handed out to those close to the new regime and did not seem to be purely reward-based. Morley was close to Cromwell due to them having several shared interests, as MacCulloch himself mentions that he was 'Cromwell's congenial fellow-bibliophile', and so it is more likely that he just wanted to give his friend some of the spoils and that there was no ulterior motive, as Jane herself was certainly not rewarded and was in a worse situation after her husband's execution.[10]

George Wyatt was one of the first to mention Jane Parker in connection with the fall of the Boleyns. He named her as a witness and called her a 'wicked wife accuser of her own husband, even to the seeking of his blood' in his book, the *Life of Queen Anne Boleigne*.[11] Wyatt's work has been given a fair amount of credit, mainly due to the fact that his father, Thomas Wyatt, knew the Boleyn family well and so it is has been assumed that he knew the events of 1536. However, Thomas was in the Tower of London himself at the time and so would not have been privy to information on the case against George Boleyn. Wyatt began his book near the end of Elizabeth I's lifetime and was written at the suggestion of her Archbishop of Canterbury and at a time when many pieces of Catholic propaganda were flooding into England, so, in response, Wyatt's book is teeming with Protestant imagery.[12] It could thus be suggested that Jane was vilified by him due to her Catholic sympathies, as she was known to be close to Henry VIII's eldest daughter, Princess Mary. Apart from this, we also need to consider the fact that George Wyatt was not born until 1553, many years after the events in question and was writing in the reign of Elizabeth I, the daughter of Henry VIII and Anne Boleyn, and so needed to find a scapegoat for Elizabeth's mother's execution. By this time, Jane had been executed for her involvement in Katherine Howard's affair with Culpepper, a 'just punishment', and so she was an easy target.[13]

Eric Ives' *The Life and Death of Anne Boleyn* perpetuates the view of Jane Parker as someone who deliberately sought Anne's downfall, as he calls her 'Anne's enemy' and makes a case for her having acted against the interests of the Boleyn family, although he struggles to come up with a reasonable explanation as to why and ignores the fact that she was in a difficult financial situation after her husband's execution.[14] Ives bases this on the words of Antony Antony and Bishop Burnet. He somewhat clumsily speculates on what Antony Antony may have said, basing this on the idea that Bishop Burnet had access to Antony's journal when he wrote his work, stating that the journal probably 'included words to the effect that 'the wife of Lord Rochford was a particular instrument in the death of Queen Anne'.[15] The word 'probably' is the problem here and, without having access to the journal ourselves, we should not speculate on what it may or may not have said. We, therefore, turn back to Bishop Burnet, whose work first appeared in 1679, who confidently stated that:

'Her [Anne's] brother, the lord Rochford, was her friend, as well as brother; but his spiteful wife was jealous of him: and, being a woman of no sort of virtue, (as will appear afterwards by her

serving queen Catharine Howard in her beastly practices, for which she was attainted and executed,) she carried many stories to the king, or some about him, to persuade, that there was a familiarity between the queen and her brother, beyond what so near a relation could justify.'[16]

Burnet's words have been given more credit than they deserve, as, if we take away the possible connection with Antony Antony's lost journal, all we are left with is another secondary source written over a hundred years after the event in question. He seems to have been influenced, like many others, by hindsight, as he mentions Jane's involvement with Katherine Howard's affair. He links her involvement and execution later on to her lack of virtue, which led to her helping Katherine 'in her beastly practices'.[17] This is a clear sign that he had let hindsight cloud his judgement.

Another source often cited for Jane's involvement in Anne Boleyn's downfall is a letter by John Husee, Lord Lisle, to his wife on 24 May 1536. He wrote about the women who accused Anne of being unfaithful to the king, stating that 'what was said was wondrous discreetly spoken: the first accusers, the Lady Worcester, and Nan Cobham, with one maid more'.[18] The 'one maid more' has been suggested to be Jane, however, Jane was a married woman, hardly a maid, and would surely have been referred to as Lady or Viscountess Rochford.

De Carles' poem is one of the most controversial sources regarding Anne Boleyn's fall, dividing historians over whether or not it should be taken at face value. Some historians, most notably G.W. Bernard, take it as such and use it to argue that Anne was guilty of adultery.[19] If we take that view, then we have to see if his words regarding a woman who accused Anne are reliable as well. De Carles' writes that in his trial, George Boleyn drew attention to the fact that the evidence against him was flimsy and that it was:

'only on the word of one woman
That you believe and use to greatly blame me,
And the effect of this presumption
Determines my condemnation.'[20]

This 'one woman' has been taken over the years to mean his wife, Jane Parker. If this was true, why did he not name her? It seems unlikely that he would spare her the shame and judgement of being known to have acted against her husband in such a way, especially if the rumours of their unhappy marriage are true. It is much more likely that he was referring to someone like Lady Worcester or Lady Wingfield, who we know gave evidence against Anne and was mentioned by name in several different primary sources, such as *The Lisle Letters* and John Spelman's reports.

However, we need to remember that Bernard is in the minority in believing Anne guilty of the charges against her and that most historians have dismissed de Carles' poem out of hand. Carles was around at the time of Anne's execution and dated his poem to June 1536, one month after the event, but it was still not published until 1545. Eric Ives informs us that the poem sticks closely to the official version of events and that the author 'wrote on the basis of what was known by the French embassy' and that it is 'in effect, the government line in translation'.[21] This seems probable, seeing how close it is to the accounts we have by Cromwell and that of the trials, which means we have to remember this when we are assessing its validity. Going on that assumption, the 'one woman' mentioned by de Carles has to be one of the women mentioned in the various official reports, either Lady Wingfield or Lady Worcester.[22] The reason why there is no name is because this is still second-hand information; the French embassy would not have needed to know the names of the individual witnesses that testified against the Boleyns. Therefore, we can dismiss the notion that the poem was referring to Jane Parker as the 'one woman' who gave evidence against George.

Another contemporary who fails to mention Jane Parker in his account is John Spelman. Spelman was a judge and wrote reports on several trials, including those of Bishop Fisher and Thomas More.[23] His reports give us some insight as to who were thought to be the chief accusers against the Boleyns, with Spelman placing significant blame on Lady Wingfield, one of Anne Boleyn's former ladies of the bedchamber, who had died several years before the trial:

> 'And all the evidence was of bawdery and lechery, so that there was no such whore in the realm. Note that this matter was disclosed by a woman called the Lady Wingfeilde, who had been a servant to the said queen and of the same qualities; and suddenly the said Wingfeilde became sick and a short time before her death showed this matter to one of her etc.'[24]

There is no mention of Jane Parker in Spelman's account of Anne Boleyn's downfall, which contradicts the idea that she was the one who provided the evidence against Anne and George. So far both Lady Worcester and Lady Wingfield have been mentioned by contemporaries, as well as an unnamed woman, but not Jane herself. Jane was a prominent figure at court, being the sister-in-law of the queen, and any scandal surrounding her and her marriage would have been reported, but the sources are silent in regards to her. Someone as important as John Spelman would not have left her out of his report if she had been involved.

The only thing Jane was guilty of is having admitted to someone, most likely Cromwell, that Anne had said to her that Henry had sexual problems. The Imperial Ambassador, Eustace Chapuys, wrote in a dispatch to Charles V that Anne 'had told his [George Boleyn's] wife that the King "nestoit habile en cas de soy copuler avec femme, et quil navoit ne vertu ne puissance."'[25] This essentially meant that Henry was unable to have sexual intercourse and thus unable to have any more children.[26] This statement was a shocking and careless one on Anne's part, but it does not mean that Jane willingly handed over this information. Julia Fox has proposed that she was tricked into revealing this and the stress of the events would not have helped matters.[27] It was very sudden and, in the words of Fox, 'there was no time to separate out what testimony might be damaging'.[28] All of Anne's women would have been interrogated and it is a believable theory that she accidentally revealed this either due to stress or presuming those interrogating her already knew. As this is the only information we know for certain she provided, it does not on its own support the idea of her willingly condemning her husband.

Jane's husband was executed on 17 May 1536, followed by his sister two days later. We do not know if Jane was there to see either of the executions, but it is likely that she saw her husband's execution at least, as she had openly supported him so far and it was a public one, unlike Anne's. He was executed before the other men and, in his speech, George said:

'O ye gentlemen and Christians, I was born under the law, and I die under the law, forasmuch as it is the law which hath condemned me... Ye gentlemen here present, I come not hither to preach unto you, but to die. Nor do I now seek for any thing, in the sorrowful plight in which I here stand, save that I may soon bathe my dry and parched lips in the living fountain of God's everlasting and infinite mercy. And I beseech you all, in his holy name, to pray unto him for me, confessing truly that I deserve death, even though I had a thousand lives - yea even to die with far more and worse shame and dishonour than hath ever been heard of before. For I am a miserable sinner, who have grievously and often times offended; nay and in very truth, I know not of any more perverse or wicked sinner than I have been up until now.'[29]

This was the standard execution speech, confessing any sins in the hope that he would be forgiven and go to Heaven, but still must have been hard for Jane to hear. It is doubtful that these were any real sins, such as homosexuality and promiscuity, as some historians have suggested, but instead was just George covering himself for whatever may await him after death. One part of his speech that must have particularly struck a cord with Jane was when he spoke about the 'flatteries of the Court, and the favours and treacheries of Fortune, which only raiseth men aloft that with so much the greater force she may dash them again upon the ground'.[30] This was an apt statement and something which Jane probably kept in mind for the rest of her time at court. It was a lion's den and no one was safe.

Chapter 6

Aftermath of the Fall of the Boleyns

'Mayster Secretory, as a power desolate widow wythoute comfort, as to my specyall trust under God and my Pryns, I have me most humbly recommendyd unto youe; prayng youe, after your accustemyd gentyll maner to all them that be in such lamentabull case as I ame in, to be meane to the Kyngs gracious Hyghnes for me for suche power stuffe and plate as my husbonde had, whome God pardon; that of hys gracious and mere lyberalyte I may have hyt to helpe me to my power lyvyng, whiche to his Hyghnes ys nothynge to be regardyd, and to me schuld be a most hygh helpe and souccor.'[1]

Jane's letter to Thomas Cromwell after the downfall of her husband and sister-in-law is a desperate one, in which she calls herself a poor 'desolate widow' and begs for financial help. These are not the words of a woman who helped bring down the Boleyn family, as she had certainly not gained from their downfall. No matter which way you look at it, the downfall of the Boleyn family was a disaster for Jane. The only thing she could hope for now was her marriage settlement, and that wouldn't come easy.

Jane's request for help from Cromwell wouldn't have been an easy one, seeing as he had spearheaded the investigation against her husband and sister-in-law, but she had nowhere else to turn. He was known for helping widows, as she mentions in her letter to him. She requested more money from her father-in-law, Thomas Boleyn, which he eventually agreed to, but not without some complaint in a letter back to Cromwell in July 1536:

'I received a letter from the King, with another from you concerning an augmentation of living to my daughter of Rochford; and although

my living of late is much decayed, I am content, whereas she now has 100 marks a year, and 200 marks a year after my decease, to give her 50 marks a year more in hand. From Lady day last past she shall have 100l. a year to live on, where she should have had only 100 marks as long as I live, and after my death 300 marks a year. Beseeching you to inform the King that I do this alonely for his pleasure. When I married I had only 50l. a year to live on for me and my wife as long as my father lived, and yet she brought me every year a child. I thank you for your goodness to me when I am far off, and cannot always be present to answer for myself. Hever, this first Sunday of July.[2]

Thomas was complaining about the fact he should have to pay so much to his now widowed daughter-in-law, yet the agreement drawn up upon her marriage to George must have stipulated that he pay a certain amount and he must have known he was in the wrong. This increase in her income would have allowed Jane to live much more comfortably, but she still now had no real purpose and was effectively in exile, away from everyone she knew at court.

It was not long before she was invited back to court to serve the new queen, a move probably made by Thomas Cromwell, but Jane knew she would have to learn how to conceal her grief. She could not express it due to her husband having been executed as a traitor, however, she was described by George Cavendish in his *Metrical Visions*, with him saying that 'I aspied a widowe in blake full woo begon'.[3] By all accounts, she continued to dress in black for the rest of her life and so continued to silently mourn a husband she may have loved or, at the very least, cared for.

Chapter 7

Serving the Third and Fourth Wives

It is hard to know the exact date Jane returned to court, but it can't have been long after Jane Seymour had become queen. We can't imagine how Jane must have felt at returning to a court that was now dominated by the Seymours, serving a new mistress, and incredibly isolated from any possible support. The remaining Boleyns would not support her, even if they wanted to, and she was now the wife of a traitor. She would only survive now by keeping her head down and learning to serve Jane Seymour as she did Anne Boleyn and Katherine of Aragon before her. Jane kept to the shadows well, so much so that it is hard to track her movements after her return to court, but we can presume that she stayed by the new queen.

Lady Mary returned to favour shortly after Jane Seymour became queen and this was one thing that Jane Parker could be happy about and, despite her connection to the Boleyn family, there is a record of several gifts being exchanged between the two, suggesting a comfortable acquaintance, if not a friendship. Mary might have even known that Jane had supported her cause even when serving Anne Boleyn and perhaps even sympathised with her current predicament. We know that Mary kept at least one of the gifts Jane gave her, as there is a record of a repair for a clock given to her:

'Itm pated for mending of the Clocke whiche my lade gee hadof my lady rochford. v s.'[1]

Mary paid five shillings (around £110) to fix a clock that Jane had previously given to her as a gift.[2] This shows that the gift obviously must have meant something to her and reveals that, despite the differences between her and the Boleyn family, she did not hold any grudge against Jane for being married into that family.

On 27 May 1537, just over a year after Anne Boleyn's execution, it was announced that Jane Seymour was pregnant. Charles Wriothesley records that a Te Deum was sung for the 'joye of the Queenes quickninge of childe'.[3] It had been a slow start, but, finally, the King's gamble seemed to be paying off. Jane had witnessed one royal birth, that of Princess Elizabeth (now Lady Elizabeth), and two miscarriages, so she had some experience of this and must have been both excited and anxious as to how this pregnancy would turn out.

On 16 September, the Queen retired to her chamber at Hampton Court Palace for her confinement. As she did with her sister-in-law, Jane would have joined the Queen for her confinement and waited anxiously for her labour to start. On Thursday 11 October, contractions began and Jane was among the ladies who must have been fervently praying for a safe delivery. It wasn't until 2 am on the Friday morning that the child was finally born – a prince at last.

The birth of Prince Edward would have brought some feeling of relief to Jane. The King now finally had a son and, at least while he survived, he was unlikely to leave his current wife. Henry was overjoyed by the birth and, if he was happy, the court could be happy. Sadly, that happiness would not last. Just eight days after the christening of Prince Edward, on 24 October 1537, Jane Seymour passed away at Hampton Court Palace. Jane Parker had probably been at the Queen's side when she died, along with her other ladies.

Jane was one of the most prominent women in Jane Seymour's funeral procession, second only to Lady Mary, who she was behind in the procession and held the train for.[4] She was one of 29 mourners, one for each year of the late Queen's life. We cannot know for certain how Jane felt about the late queen, but we can guess that she must have felt some pity for the woman who had finally given Henry what he wanted, only to die before she reaped any of the real benefits of being in the king's favour and firm in her position as mother of the heir.

Jane Parker's future was now once again uncertain, with no queen to serve, there was no reason for there to continue to be ladies-in-waiting at court, and so they were soon disbanded. She had become successful at court, marked by the fact she was given a New Year's gift by the late Queen in 1537, and this step into the unknown again must have been daunting.[5] Her status had remained intact since the fall of her husband. She was still a viscountess, using the title of Lady Rochford, but there was now the prospect of her leaving court for good. For once, there was no queen waiting in the wings and as such there was no need for her to stay.

While away from court, Jane was once again involved in some negotiations with her father-in-law over her jointure. Julia Fox has researched this matter thoroughly, piecing together different sources, and it is her we turn to for information regarding these negotiations. After his wife's death, Thomas Boleyn started putting his own affairs in order and started looking into the matter of selling some property, the manors of Aylesbury and Bierton in Buckinghamshire, several of which Jane had a right to as part of her settlement. Jane did not have ownership of the manors outright, but she had a life interest in them and had to be consulted before any sale took place. In exchange for giving up those manors, Thomas offered her the manor of Swavesey in Cambridgeshire.[6] Fox then tells us that:

'The situation was complicated further because Jane schemed to obtain a private Act of Parliament as a form of insurance policy. She was no fool, she knew just how sharp Thomas could be if money was at stake, and she also knew that he was ageing. Should he die before the entire deal came to fruition, there was no way of knowing

whether it would be honoured.'[7]

Jane had grown from the naïve young woman she had been when she first arrived at court, she knew how to play the game now and protect herself. She was able to obtain an Act of Parliament from the King, probably with the help of Cromwell yet again, and secure the manor of Swavesey from Thomas Boleyn. With Thomas' death in March 1539, she was also entitled to the Boleyn family seat of Blickling and held onto it for the remainder of her life.[8]

A couple of years after Jane Seymour's death, the news that many, including Jane, had been waiting for finally came – Henry VIII was to marry again. It was 1539 and the woman chosen was Anne of Cleves, the first foreign match since Katherine of Aragon, and a woman that the King hadn't even set eyes on yet. At some point in that year, we have no precise date for it, Jane was appointed to serve the new queen. Most of the women appointed to serve Anne would have been familiar to Jane, as they had served the previous queens, but there was one new face, that of the Duke of Norfolk's niece, the young Katherine Howard.

Jane met the new queen sometime after she arrived in England and the culture difference would have been shocking. Anne was dressed very differently to the English ladies and not very flatteringly, she also did not speak English and so Jane would have found it difficult to communicate with her and break the language barrier.

Anne of Cleves and Henry VIII's marriage did not go smoothly and, after six months together, it was clear that the King wanted an annulment. The annulment required evidence from both sides in order for it to go smoothly and to avoid the multitude of problems that had befallen Henry's attempt to annul his first marriage. We know that Jane was a participant in an intimate and important conversation with Anne of Cleves about her marriage to Henry and its consummation, or lack of. This implies that Anne grasped English relatively quickly, enough for Jane to enquire as to her nightly activities with the King. After Katherine Edgecomb, one of Anne's ladies-in-waiting, suggested that she was still a maid, Jane agreed, stating that 'By our Lady, Madam, I think your Grace is a mayd still, indede'.[9] Anne replied by asking how could she still be a maid and yet sleep every night with the King. Jane answered that there 'must be more than that', leading the naïve Queen to describe the King's nightly activities as such:

> 'Why, said she, when he comes to bed he kisses me, and taketh me by the hand, and byddeth me, Good night, swete hart: and in the morning kisses me, and byddeth me, Farewel, darlyng. Is not thys enough?'[10]

From this statement, it appears that the Queen led a sheltered life and not to have grasped what was meant to happen in the marriage bed. She had unwittingly revealed a crucial piece of information to her ladies and, had it not already been the subject of court gossip, Jane could have guessed that the King was displeased with his new queen and that she would not last long at this rate. She may have even worried for her position, as there was no need for her without a queen at court, and she would be back in limbo as she had been after Jane Seymour's death.

This suggests that Anne had grasped the English language very quickly, which seems unlikely, as well as the fact she wasn't prepared at all by her mother, as was the norm, as to what to expect on her wedding night. Perhaps Anne's ladies were saying this as they thought it was what the King wanted to hear? This would have proved that the relationship was not consummated and so could be annulled. Jane knew what happened to people who stood in Henry VIII's way and may have done what she could to make the process go more smoothly.

Jane's testimony as to the conversation with Anne of Cleves was crucial to the annulment. In July 1540, the short marriage of Henry and Anne was annulled and she was awarded a generous settlement, including a place Jane would have been very familiar with, Hever Castle in Kent. This was the former Boleyn family home and to see it go to another Anne, another wife of Henry VIII, must have been odd, to say the least.

Jane had now seen four of Henry VIII's wives come and go, either through annulment, execution or natural death, and must have felt by now that things would never settle. Could she bear to hope that the next wife would fare any better than the last?

Chapter 8

Confidante to Katherine Howard

It turns out that, as with Katherine of Aragon and Anne Boleyn years before, Henry VIII had another woman waiting in the wings and wasted no time in making his move once the annulment from Anne of Cleves was official. It must have felt like history repeating itself for Jane. Henry VIII married his fifth queen, the young Katherine Howard, on 28 July 1540, just a few weeks after the annulment from his fourth wife. We do not know Katherine's exact age, as she was born before parish records were made mandatory, so we can only estimate based on what little we have available. Two of her latest biographers put forward convincing arguments for the mid-1520s, with Gareth Russell favouring between 1522 and 1523 and Josephine Wilkinson favouring 1525.[1] This would make her between 15 and 18 years old when she married the 49-year-old king. She had little experience of court, having only served under Anne of Cleves, who had only been married to Henry for six months, and so naturally would have looked to someone more experienced to guide her. Jane Parker was the obvious choice for a companion and mentor to the younger woman.

Jane may have known that Katherine was to be Henry's next queen, as Anne certainly knew Henry was having an affair with her, as she had mentioned it to the Cleves ambassador, and gossip could spread like wildfire at court.[2] Katherine Howard's relationship with the King was in stark contrast to his relationship with Anne of Cleves. He was besotted with his young queen, full of passion and, thankfully, there was no need for a repeat of the conversation Jane had with Anne over the non-consummation of her marriage. As long as Henry was happy, those around him could breathe a sigh of relief.

On the same day of Henry and Katherine's marriage, Thomas Cromwell was executed. This would have been a blow to Jane, as she lost her protector and the one person who had been her advocate since she lost her husband. Despite the role he had in the downfall of her husband, his fall from grace was swift and would have been shocking and perhaps even upsetting to Jane. It would have been a stark reminder of the dangers of Henry VIII's court. However, she soon found a new protector in that of the young queen, but she could not possibly imagine where that new relationship would take her.

Gareth Russell in his book Young and Damned and Fair has suggested that Katherine and Jane grew close due to their 'love of scandal and intrigue'.[3] This theory is based on the fact that Jane had previously assisted with trying to remove one of Henry VIII's mistresses for Anne Boleyn, as discussed in the previous chapter, and so Russell suggests that the two may have been naturally drawn to each other. He states:

'The reasons for this unusual and damaging friendship are therefore difficult to determine, but given what happened next and what we know of both ladies' personalities, it does seem as if a shared love of scandal and intrigue brought them together – a conclusion supported by the fact that Jane was instrumental in arranging Catherine's secret Maundy meeting with Culpepper.'[4]

This is a rather simplistic explanation and, seeing how Jane struggled after her husband's execution, any love of scandal would have to be weighed up with the immense danger court intrigue posed. She may have enjoyed it before Anne Boleyn's execution, but no queen had been executed back then and the prospect would have been unthinkable. It seems more likely that Katherine sought out someone who had the most experience of the court, as she had only been there a short time, serving under Anne of Cleves, whereas Jane had served all of Henry VIII's past queens.

Whatever the reason, it wasn't long before Jane was elevated above the rest of Katherine's women, proving the new queen's favour of her. She was increasingly spending more and more time with the Queen in private and was asked to do something that would lead to her eventual downfall – organise a meeting with Thomas Culpepper.

Thomas Culpepper had been in some kind of relationship with Katherine Howard before she married the King, during her time serving Anne of Cleves, which seems to have ended with Culpepper becoming interested in another woman. However, despite her marriage, he soon started pursuing Katherine again. It appears that Jane helped arrange a meeting between the two, in which the Queen gave Culpepper a velvet cap.[5] Jane seems to have organised several meetings between the couple, with later evidence given by Katherine's other ladies-in-waiting providing crucial information. Their accounts frequently mention being suspicious about Katherine's close relationship with Jane. The most detailed account was given by Margaret Morton, one of Katherine's chamberers, which includes much detail she includes on Jane's role in organising meetings between her and Culpepper:

'She never mistrusted the Queen until at Hatfeld she saw her look out of her chamber window on Mr. Culpeper after such sort that she thought there was love between them. There the Queen gave order that neither Mrs. Lofkyng "nor no nother" should come into her bedchamber unless called. At Lodyngton she carried a sealed letter, without superscription, to my lady of Rochford, to whom the Queen bade her say she was sorry that she could write no better. Lady Rochford promised an answer next morning, which deponent was sent for and brought, with a message "praying her Grace to keep it secret and not to lay it abroad." After Kath. Tylnay came, the Queen could not abide Mrs. Loffken or deponent. Thinks "my

*lade off Rochfor the prynsy a casyoun off har ffoley." At Pomfrat the
Queen was angry with Mrs. Loffkyn and her and threatened to put
them away. If they had gone she thinks the Queen would have taken
others of Lady Rochford's putting. She confesses all that she said to
Mr. Comptroller, and also that at Pomfret, every night, the Queen,
being alone with lady Rochford, locked and bolted her chamber door
on the inside, and Mr. Dane, sent to the Queen from the King, one
night found it bolted."[6]*

This 'sealed letter' that the Queen gave to Jane is an interesting
detail to note. On the face of it, it could just be a harmless
message from the Queen to one of her servants, however, it
was significant enough for it to be noticed and remembered by
one of her ladies later on. It is implied that this is the letter to
Thomas Culpepper that was later found in his possessions and
used as evidence against the couple.[7] Katherine mentions Jane
directly in the letter, saying for Culpepper to come 'when my
lady Rochforthe is here', and that supports Margaret Morton's
version of events, in which Jane was alone with Katherine and,
Morton guesses, Culpepper.[8]

Now, why did Jane become involved in this affair in the
first place? Some people have accused Jane of using Katherine
Howard's interest in Thomas Culpepper to further her own
agenda or even to get herself out of some trouble she had got
into during her time serving Anne of Cleves, explaining her
recklessness in participating in such a scheme. Retha Warnicke
is one such historian and states that Culpepper was 'bribing
Lady Rochford to assist him in obtaining political control of
Katherine'.[9] But bribing her with what? It would have to be
something serious for her to put herself in such danger and
Warnicke does not give us an explanation for why she thinks
this. As we have seen, Warnicke has no good opinion of Jane and
so, without her providing any evidence and with her supporting
the myth of Jane's actions against the Boleyns, this theory holds

no real weight.

David Starkey in his book Six Wives: The Queens of Henry VIII tentatively puts forward the suggestion that Jane might have been 'living out in Catherine the romantic fantasies that she had never known'.[10] The fact that Thomas Culpepper later blames Jane for his affair with Katherine Howard, saying that 'Lady Rochford provoked him much to love the Queen', supports Starkey's suggestion that she wanted to bring the two together romantically.[11] Nevertheless, this suggestion solely rests on the idea that she had an unhappy marriage to George Boleyn, the evidence for which was disproved earlier on in this book, and so is not worth seriously considering.

Julia Fox's theory as to why Jane became involved in such a dangerous affair seems to be the most credible one, with her writing that it most likely started off as an innocent request from the Queen to her senior lady-in-waiting and then escalated from there.[12] Once Jane became involved, she could not distance herself from events for fear of condemning herself and had no powerful faction at court, as Katherine did with the Howard family, to support her if she faced her wrath. Although we will never know for sure what drove Jane to decide to act as Katherine's confidant and as an intercessor for the couple, this is the most plausible explanation.

So Jane probably became involved unwillingly, unsure as to the exact nature of Katherine's relationship with Culpepper, and was soon in too deep to get out. Instead, she just had to do her best to protect the young woman and make sure she wasn't caught.

After the initial meeting, Culpepper and Katherine did not meet again in private for some time, as he did not seem grateful of her gift of the velvet cap and she had made it clear she no longer wanted to see him. Around the same time as this meeting, Katherine may have fallen pregnant by the King. The first mention we have of a possible pregnancy is by Ambassador

Marillac in one of his dispatches. He wrote on 10 April 1541 that:

'this Queen is thought to be with child, which would be a very great joy to this King, who, it seems, believes it, and intends, if it be found true, to have her crowned at Whitsuntide. Already all the embroiderers that can be got are employed making furniture and tapestry, the copes and ornaments taken from the churches not being spared. Moreover, the young lords and gentlemen of this Court are practising daily for the jousts and tournaments to be then made.'[13]

This would have been a big moment for Jane, as she had the best relationship with one of Henry VIII's wives since Anne Boleyn had been executed. She was firm in her position at court and any child Katherine bore Henry would have only made her position stronger. As much as a son would be preferred, the King at least already had one son and any more children at his time of life from his 'rose without a thorn' would have been a blessing. However, Jane must have had the death of Jane Seymour in the back of her mind too and so would have been all too aware of the dangers of childbirth.

Yet, despite a few reports of preparations being made for the rumoured child, after a few months, it all went quiet. Whether Katherine had a miscarriage or was simply mistaken we cannot know for sure, but it would have been a huge disappointment for the royal couple. Katherine's coronation was put on hold indefinitely and no more was said on the subject. Gareth Russell suggests that she may have even invented the story of her pregnancy 'in order to restore herself to the King's favour after the upset their relationship had suffered during his spell of poor health' and that she hoped to turn the lie into truth when possible.[14] This seems possible, as Katherine was young, naïve and perhaps a little unsure of her security in the King's affections, but would have been a dangerous strategy had it been the case. Jane would have been the closest person to Katherine and, from her experience with Henry's previous wives, would have been likely to know the truth of the matter. It is interesting to speculate just how involved Jane was in this if Katherine had been pretending to be pregnant.

Whatever the case, Katherine soon had other matters on her mind. Thomas Culpepper continued to make advances towards her and the Queen noticed him staring at her, even after she said she wanted nothing more to do with him. When she brought this up with Jane, she answered 'yet must yow gyff men leave to looke for they woll looke uppon yowe'.[15] Jane was telling Katherine that she was in the public eye now and could not get upset about one man looking at her and must control her anger towards him and not let it show.

Sometime in either May or June, Culpepper fell sick and because of this Katherine could no longer stay mad at him. She sent dinners to his rooms on several occasions and struggled to control her feelings for him.[16] It was not long before she gave in and had need of Jane again to act as intercessor.

While on progress, we have a record of a strange conversation between Katherine and one of the ladies, Katherine Tilney, in which she tells her to find Jane and ask her 'when she should have the thing she promised her' and Jane answered that she 'sat up for it, and she would next day bring her word herself'.[17] She had reported that she had been sent multiple strange messages to give to Jane recently and that she knew not 'how to utter them'.

Katherine Tilney also reported under interrogation that the Queen went to Jane's chamber twice while on the same progress, which she says was 'up a little pair of stairs by the Queen's chamber'.[18] Katherine Tilney and Margaret, another one of the Queen's ladies, followed her to Jane's chamber but were sent away. Margaret checked again a little while later and then, when she went to bed, around 2 am:

'examinate [Katherine Tilney] said, "Jesus, is not the Queen abed yet?" She replied, "Yes, even now." The second night the Queen sent the rest to bed and took examinate with her, but she was in a little place with Lady Rochford's [Jane's] woman and could not tell who came into Lady Rochford's chamber.'[19]

Jane had stayed with the Queen until at least 2 am one night and again another night, although we do not know what the two and, presumably, Culpepper got up to. By now, Jane was very close to Katherine and in way too deep to get out again without extreme difficulty. So she seems to have embraced her role as a chaperone, mother figure and confidante. She told her that another man was also interested in her, Thomas Paston, but by this time Katherine only had eyes for Culpepper.[20]

There is also an interesting report of secret letters passing between Jane and the Queen, with Margaret confessing that she:

'carried a sealed letter, without superscription, to my lady of Rochford [Jane], to whom the Queen bade her say she was sorry that she could write no better. Lady Rochford promised an answer next morning, which deponent [Margaret] was sent for and brought, with a message "praying her Grace to keep it secret and not to lay it abroad."'[21]

This close relationship the Queen had with Jane was the source of much jealousy and suspicion within the household, with them thinking Jane had too much influence over her. This is evident later on in Margaret's confession, in which she states that:

'At Pomfrat the Queen was angry with Mrs. Loffkyn and her and threatened to put them away. If they had gone she thinks the Queen would have taken others of Lady Rochford's putting. She confesses all that she said to Mr. Comptroller, and also that at Pomfret, every night, the Queen, being alone with lady Rochford, locked and bolted

her chamber door on the inside, and Mr. Dane, sent to the Queen
from the King, one night found it bolted.'[22]

Margaret must have thought Jane had the power to install her
own ladies in the place of her and others, although it is highly
unlikely she had that much power. She was close to the Queen,
as we can see, but she was already aware of how much attention
she was drawing to herself and wouldn't want to do anything
else to put the spotlight on her.

Jane's own confession gives us much insight into how she
viewed the matter and how reckless Katherine was becoming.
She describes one of the late-night meetings at Lincoln, in which:

'she and the Queen were at the back door waiting for Culpeper, at
11 p.m., when one of the watch came with a light and locked the
door. Shortly after Culpeper came in, saying he and his man had
picked the lock. Since her trouble the Queen has daily asked for
Culpeper, saying that if that matter came not out she feared not.'[23]

The two women must have been so close to having been caught.
As previously mentioned, other servants had also found on a
different occasion the Queen's door bolted when it shouldn't
have been. These close encounters must have been terrifying,
even more so as Katherine seemed not to be worried about being
caught, as she 'feared not' the matter coming out. This was
becoming more and more dangerous, how long would it be until
they were found out?

Chapter 9

The Downfall of Katherine Howard and Jane Parker

On some level, Jane must have known she would have been caught eventually. It was just a matter of time. On 2 November 1541, Henry VIII was given a letter by Thomas Cranmer, the Archbishop of Canterbury, who alerted him to a previous relationship Katherine Howard was alleged to have had with Francis Dereham while she was under the care of the Dowager Duchess of Norfolk.[1] This letter was received just a day after the King had been praising his queen and had asked the Bishop of Lincoln to pray for her and give thanks with him. Not long before Henry had marvelled that he had obtained 'such a jewel for womanhod' and praised her 'vertue and good bihavor'.[2] This was a shock to the King, who originally refused to believe the accusations against his beloved young queen, but allowed the investigation to proceed regardless. Despite not having been involved in the affair with Francis Dereham, any investigation into the Queen's activities would have terrified Jane, as she knew that one slip up could bring her world crashing down around her.

On 7 November, the Queen was confined to her chambers, along with her ladies, Jane included. One by one they were questioned, although, at first Jane would not have been questioned in regards to Katherine's conduct. She had not known Francis Dereham prior to his arrival at court and so could not really speak on the matter. She was only brought to the attention of the officials once Culpepper's name was brought up and the suspicious activities she had been getting up to regarding him and Katherine.

Under interrogation on around 11 or 12 November 1541,

Thomas Culpepper described his first meeting with Katherine, in which she 'gave him a velvet cap' and clearly states that 'Lady Rochford contrived these interviews'.[3] All three of those involved made no secret of Jane's involvement in organising these meetings but do not tell us why she became involved in the first place, putting herself at great risk.

Katherine Howard's first confession about her relationship with Thomas Culpepper, which was made on 12 November, is difficult to decipher and figure out what to take seriously, as it claims that Jane instigated the affair between her and Culpepper. It is similar to Culpepper's accusation against Jane, but it is much more detailed than his account, as it asserts that Jane:

> 'hath sondry tymez made instans to her to speke with Culpeper declaring hym to beare her good wyll and favour, wheruppon she did at the last graunte he shuld speke with her, my lady of Rocheford affyrmyng that he desiered nothyng ells but to speke with her and that she durst swere upon a booke he ment nothing but honestye.'[4]

This account was after Katherine's first confession, in which no mention is made of Jane, however at that point the king's men were only interested in her relationship with Francis Dereham, which Jane had no part in. Of course, we have to take all confessions with a pinch of salt, as those making them are trying to save themselves, so we need to look at the common links between the accounts to verify the details. Culpepper, Katherine and Morton all mention Jane in their accounts, so we do know that she was involved in some way, unlike the myth of her involvement in the events of 1536. However, it is highly unlikely she instigated the affair, as Katherine and Culpepper assert. Jane was a convenient person to blame, being a servant and the third person in the affair, with no one to defend her. She was, in Julia Fox's words, an easy target for Katherine, as she was a woman 'whose own husband, according to Henry and the judgement of the courts, had thought nothing of having an incestuous relationship with his whore of a sister; anything, therefore, could be believed of her'.[5]

Those investigating the affair did not fall for Katherine's story that she was the puppet of her senior lady-in-waiting and neither should we. Jane may have helped later on and she may have seemed willing, but most likely was trying to keep on Katherine's good side and ensure they were not caught. This view has been supported by David Loades, as he writes that Jane could have been 'aware that the queen was a light-headed young woman, and that her activities needed some sort of control'.[6] This is further supported by the fact that Jane was reported to have actively looked for meeting places in advance whilst on the 1541 northern progress with the court.[7]

There is generally not much credit given to Jane Parker's account of events, due to the fact that she was said to be insane, but she was coherent enough to provide a full statement and one that was in fact very similar to Katherine's account, so it should not be dismissed out of hand. Her assertion that she was involved but had 'heard or saw nothing of what passed' between Katherine and Culpepper is unlikely, seeing as she was only at the other end of the room according to her confession, and shows someone who was scared of death and trying to save herself, as most would try to do in that situation.[8] Claiming ignorance was one of the only weapons at her disposal and she tried to stress her ignorance by even saying that she fell asleep during one of the meetings, but her efforts are undermined by her last statement, in which she says that she 'thinks Culpeper has known the Queen carnally'.[9] Not hearing or even falling asleep during such a time would have been near impossible, not least because of the very real danger of being caught that was hanging over the three of them. Jane's statement about the nature of Katherine's relationship with Culpepper could, however, hint at her unstable mental state, as her confession is confusing and contradicts itself. If she was showing signs of mental illness at this stage, it is not a stretch to say that it may have influenced her decision to help Katherine and Culpepper in the first place.

Jane's statement that she 'heard or saw nothing' of what happened as 'the Queen was at the other end of the room and Culpeper on the stairs' is supported somewhat by Katherine Howard's first confession over Culpepper, in which she states that 'when Culpeper was talkyng with hir my lady Rocheford wold many tymez, being ever by, sytt sumwhatt farre of or turn hyr bak and she wold sey to her "For Goddes sake madam even nere us."'[10] Katherine saying that Jane was 'sumwhatt farre of' from her when she met with Culpepper, enough for her to be chided for it and to be told to move closer, does support Jane's assertion that she 'heard or saw nothing', yet she still must have been close enough to hear that and therefore close enough to hear what was going on between the couple. This move on Jane's part must have been deliberate, so that she could deny all knowledge of what happened later on. This suggests that any symptoms of a nervous breakdown that presented in her later on were not present when she decided to help arrange these meetings.

One argument as to why Jane became involved is because she was not thinking straight, mainly due to a mental illness or nervous breakdown. The Imperial Ambassador, Eustace Chapuys, is the first to report on Jane Parker's nervous breakdown, writing in a letter to the Emperor in December 1541 about the proceedings against Katherine, Jane and the men involved and writes in some detail about Jane's madness:

> 'Dame de Rochefort [Jane] would have been sentenced at the same time had she not, on the third day after her imprisonment, been seized with a fit of madness (frenesi) by which her brain is affected... True it is that now and then she recovers her reason, and that the King takes care that his own physicians visit her daily, for he desires her recovery chiefly that he may afterwards have her

executed as an example and warning to others.'[11]

There has been some doubt cast about Jane's descent into madness shortly after she was arrested, with some suggesting that the normal hysteria over proceedings was exaggerated or perhaps even faked by Jane herself in order to avoid execution, including in a recent study of Katherine Howard by Conor Byrne, in which he questions Jane's 'supposed insanity' and argues, albeit with no evidence to back him up, that it is something we should reconsider.[12] However, none of Anne Boleyn's ladies were executed alongside her in 1536 and so at that point there was no precedent for it. Jane did not know that she would be executed alongside Katherine, although there was a real chance, as none of her sister-in-law's women had. Jane also deteriorated very quickly, with Chapuys recording that she was 'seized with a fit of madness' on the third day of her imprisonment. At that point there was no telling which way proceedings would go, as they were initially focusing on Katherine's relationship with Francis Dereham, and so, if she was faking, it was a premature move. In reality, it is understandable that she should have a nervous breakdown, after what happened to her husband and sister-in-law in similar circumstances to Katherine Howard's. Her breakdown must have been convincing enough, otherwise Henry would not have sent his own physicians to nurse her back to health so that she could eventually be executed alongside her mistress. She did, however, recover when she was told she was going to die. Whether, like Gareth Russell suggests, 'the sentence shocked her into sanity', we will never know, but that brief period of madness was real enough to those around her.[13] The fact that she recovered after having been taken away from the Tower of London and allowed to rest at Lord Russell's house instead is a telling one, in that the location and the fact that her sister-in-law and husband were buried nearby in St Peter ad Vincula, where she would eventually join them, further weakened a possibly already fragile mental state.[14] No one questioned whether her madness was real at the time and Jane had been under much strain, having served a queen who had been executed and now likely to be executed alongside another one.

Why Jane Parker became involved in Katherine Howard's relationship with Thomas Culpepper will never be fully known or understood, but the previous chapter has shown that it was most likely an accident and that she became involved without knowing the full extent of what she was getting into. The letter Katherine gave her to give to Culpepper may have seemed innocent enough but, once she was involved in such a way, it was difficult to distance herself from events. She then had to make the best of the situation and tried to balance both helping Katherine keep her affair with Culpepper a secret, most notably by finding places for them to meet, and by trying to keep a distance so that she could feign ignorance if they did get caught. These were not the actions of a mad woman, as has previously been suggested, but that does not mean that she did not become mad once the affair was found out. Her sister-in-law had been executed on false charges for what Katherine did and, despite none of her ladies having been executed alongside her, the stress of the situation could have very well led to a nervous breakdown. Her confession was confused and contradictory, a possible sign of her nervous state of mind.

In mid-November, Jane's inventory was taken:

'List of plate (7 items), apparel (11 items, one "a little steel casket with a purse and forty pounds in it"), and jewels (8 items, viz., "a broach with an ag[ate], a cross of diamo[nds] with three pearls pendant, a flower of rubies, a flower with a ruby and a great emerald with a pearl pen[dent], a tablet of gold with black, green, and white enamelled, a pair of bracelets of red cornelyns, a pair of beads of gold and stones, a broach of gold with an antique head and a white face."'[15]

This was an ominous sign and the noose around Jane's neck was growing tighter and tighter. Shortly after, on 1 December 1541, Thomas Culpepper and Francis Dereham were tried for treason and found guilty, firmly sealing the fates of Katherine and Jane. They were beheaded on 10 December, although it is uncertain as to when Jane would have found out about this.

After Jane was nursed back to health, an Act of Attainder was passed in January 1542 in which the two women were sentenced to death. There was no trial for either of them. They were separately taken back to the Tower of London to await execution. This was set for 13 February. The two women were housed in separate chambers and left to make their final confessions and preparations for their souls. We cannot help but speculate what Jane must have been feeling, being in the same situation as her husband and sister-in-law, knowing what was to come.

On 13 February, the two women were taken down to be executed. Katherine was first and Jane thankfully did not have to witness it, but she would have been very aware of what was taking place. She had already seen George's and probably Anne Boleyn's executions, so knew in graphic detail what had happened to her former mistress and what was about to happen to her. Water would have been thrown over the scaffold to clean up some of the blood and fresh straw would have been laid down, so there would be little evidence of what had just happened, as Jane approached the scaffold. We do not know what she said, but we do have some detail of her execution and some idea of her speech from a letter that Ottwell Johnson wrote on 15 February 1542, which is worth quoting in full:

'And for news from hence, know ye, that, even according to my writing on Sunday last, I see the Queen and the lady Retcheford suffer within the Tower, the day following; whose souls (I doubt not) be with God, for they made the most godly and Christians' end that ever was heard tell of (I think) since the world's creation, uttering

their lively faith in the blood of Christ only, with wonderful patience and constancy to the death, and, with goodly words and steadfast countenance, they desired all Christian people to take regard unto their worthy and just punishment with death, for their offences against God heinously from their youth upward, in breaking of all his commandments, and also against the King's royal majesty very dangerously; wherefor they, being justly condemned (as they said), by the laws of the realm and Parliament, to die, required the people (I say) to take example at them for amendment of their ungodly lives, and gladly obey the King in all things, for whose preservation they did heartily pray, and willed all people so to do, commending their souls to God and earnestly calling for mercy upon Him, whom J beseech to give us grace with such faith, hope, and charity, at our departing out of this miserable world, to come to the fruition of his Godhead in joy everlasting. Amen."[16]

Jane Parker was buried in the Chapel of St. Peter ad Vincula, reunited with her husband and sister-in-law in death. She had navigated the perils of the court for many years, survived being the widow of a traitor and having served five of Henry VIII's six wives, but could not escape her fate.

Conclusion

The character of Jane Parker has been slandered over the years for little reason, with many notable historians, such as Eric Ives and Retha Warnicke, accusing her of acting against the Boleyn family and using Katherine Howard's interest in Thomas Culpepper to further her own agenda, yet the evidence simply does not support this. Jane did not deliberately seek out the downfall of the Boleyn family, which would have been against her best interests, and the small piece of evidence she did provide was not enough on its own to condemn them and was most likely given under the stress of interrogation.

For many years Jane has been blamed for, or, at the very least, connected with Anne Boleyn's downfall and execution in 1536. It has been mentioned numerous times that she willingly approached Thomas Cromwell with evidence against Anne, with historians such as Retha Warnicke suggesting that this was down to an unhappy relationship with her husband, George Boleyn, but there is little to no evidence for this. They may not have had children together but producing children does not always mean a happy marriage and it is far more likely that one or both of them had fertility problems, coupled with the fact that George was often away from court on diplomatic missions. The idea of her being jealous of his relationship with Anne is only credible if we believe the allegations of incest, which have been widely discredited and so not believed by the majority of historians. George is also not likely to have been homosexual, as Warnicke has suggested, and, as no scandal was reported, not even by Eustace Chapuys who was known for reporting gossip, George and Jane probably had a normal, even boring, relationship.

We will never know exactly how and why this myth of Jane came about, but the best guess is that she was a convenient scapegoat for the likes of George Wyatt and Bishop Burnet, with her later involvement with Katherine Howard's affair making her an easy target. Wyatt had the most motive for blaming Jane, as he was writing in the reign of Elizabeth I and so could not blame her father, Henry VIII, for her mother's execution. Jane's reputation was already sullied by her execution alongside Katherine Howard, and her being close to the Catholic Princess Mary did not help matters. In his eyes, she was a traitor and so easy to blame for another queen's death.

It is highly unlikely that Jane willingly became involved in Katherine Howard's affair with Thomas Culpepper, as she had seen first-hand how dangerous the court could be. Julia Fox's theory is the most believable, which suggests that Jane got caught up in events, perhaps with something innocent such as giving a letter to Culpepper from Katherine, and soon was in too deep to get out. She then had to cover herself and that explains why she sought out places for Katherine to meet Culpepper. Her madness was not faked, as has been suggested in the past, however she did not become involved in Katherine's affair because of that madness either. The immense strain of being interrogated near where her sister-in-law and husband were buried should not be underestimated, as it could break the most stable of people.

Jane Parker has been and likely always will be something of an enigma to historians, as we have very few pieces of evidence on her, including only one or two letters, and do not even have a verified portrait of her. She is an elusive character, always in the shadows, despite how close she was to some of the most powerful people at Henry VIII's court. However, that does not mean that we should fall into the habit of stereotyping her and assuming that the negative views of her perpetuated by later writers are accurate. There is no evidence for her deliberately acting against her husband and sister in law and very little to say that she encouraged Katherine Howard's actions. The problem is in the insistence of recent authors, both academic and popular, to explain events and find evidence where there is none, leading to the negative portrayal of Jane becoming more and more exaggerated. This book has assessed this problem and hopes that this myth of the malicious Jane Parker will be corrected in future.

References

Abbreviations

BL	British Library
Cal	Calendar
Dom	Domestic
Eccles. Mems	Ecclesiastical Memorials
fo	folio
HMC	Historical Manuscripts Commission
LP	Letters and Papers of the Reign of Henry VIII
MS	Manuscript
PPC	Proceedings of the Privy Council
pt	part
SP	State Papers
Span	Spanish
vol	volume

Introduction

1. George Wyatt, 'Extracts from the Life of Queen Anne Boleigne', in *The Life of Cardinal Wolsey*, by George Cavendish (London: Harding and Lepard, 1827), pp. 417-50 (p. 446).

2. Eric Ives, *The Life and Death of Anne Boleyn* (Oxford: Blackwell, 2006), p. 194; Lacey Baldwin Smith, *A Tudor Tragedy: The Life and Times of Catherine Howard* (London: Jonathan Cape, 1961), p. 167.

Chapter 1: Early Life

1. David Starkey, 'An Attendant Lord? Henry Parker, Lord Morley', in *'Triumphs of English': Henry Parker, Lord Morley, Translator to the Tudor Court: New Essays in Interpretation*, ed. by Marie Axton and James P. Carley (London: British Library, 2000), pp. 1-25 (p. 2).

2. Doyne C. Bell, *Notices of the Historic Persons Buried in the*

Chapel of St. Peter ad Vincula, in the Tower of London (London: John Murray, 1877), p. 27.

3. Clare Cherry and Claire Ridgway, *George Boleyn: Tudor Poet, Courtier & Diplomat* (Spain: MadeGlobal Publishing, 2014), p. 16.

4. 'Parishes: Great Hallingbury', in *A History of the County of Essex*, ed. by W. R. Powell and others (London, 1983), VIII, 113-24 <https://www.british-history.ac.uk/vch/essex/vol8/pp113-124>.

5. See *Chapter Two: At Henry VIII's Court* for the estimated date Jane was sent to court.

Chapter 2: At Henry VIII's Court

1. *The Chronicle of Calais in the Reigns of Henry VII and Henry VIII to the Year 1540*, ed. by John Gough Nichols (London: Camden Society, 1846), p. 25.

2. Anne Somerset, *Ladies in Waiting: From the Tudors to the Present Day* (London: Phoenix, 2005), p. 13.

3. Ibid., p. 14.

4. Somerset, p. 14; 'Currency Converter', *The National Archives*, 2017 <http://www.nationalarchives.gov.uk/currency-converter/> [accessed 7 February 2019].

5. Edward Hall, *Hall's Chronicle Containing the History of England, during the Reign of Henry the Fourth, and the Succeeding Monarchs, to the End of the Reign of Henry the Eighth* (London: J. Johnson, 1809), p. 631.

6. Ives, *The Life and Death of Anne Boleyn* (Oxford: Blackwell, 2006), p. 37.

Chapter 3: Marriage

1. LP, iv. 1939 (12); Julia Fox, *Jane Boleyn: The Infamous Lady Rochford* (London: Weidenfeld & Nicolson, 2008), p.39.

2. Fox, p.39.

3. BL, Royal MS, 20, B.XXI, fo.2.

4. Retha Warnicke, *The Rise and Fall of Anne Boleyn: Family Politics at the Court of Henry VIII*, Canto (Cambridge: Cambridge University Press, 1993), p. 219.
5. BL, Royal MS, 20, B.XXI, fos.98, 101.
6. Warnicke, *The Rise and Fall of Anne Boleyn*, p. 219.
7. Clare Cherry and Claire Ridgway, *George Boleyn: Tudor Poet, Courtier & Diplomat* (Spain: MadeGlobal Publishing, 2014), p. 261.
8. Anthony S. G. Edwards, 'George Cavendish's Metrical Visions: An Edition, with Introduction, Commentary and Appendices' (unpublished doctoral thesis, Birbeck College, 1975), p. 192 <https://ethos.bl.uk/OrderDetails.do?uin=uk. bl.ethos.454391?> [accessed 24 November 2018]

Chapter 4: Serving Anne Boleyn

1. LP, iv. ii. 4383.
2. LP, iv. ii. 4403.
3. LP, iv. ii. 4409.
4. Edward Hall, *Hall's Chronicle Containing the History of England, during the Reign of Henry the Fourth, and the Succeeding Monarchs, to the End of the Reign of Henry the Eighth* (London: J. Johnson, 1809), p. 794.
5. LP, vi. 613.
6. LP, vi. 419.
7. LP, x. 1251.
8. For more information on Jane's father, see *'Triumphs of English': Henry Parker, Lord Morley, Translator to the Tudor Court: New Essays in Interpretation*, ed. by Marie Axton and James P. Carley (London: British Library, 2000).
9. Ives, *The Life and Death of Anne Boleyn* (Oxford: Blackwell, 2006), p. 184.
10. LP, vii. 114.
11. LP, vii. 958.
12. LP, vii. 1257.

Chapter 5: The Downfall of Anne and George Boleyn

1. Fox, p. 348.
2. LP, ix. 566.
3. Ibid.
4. Lauren Mackay, *Among the Wolves of Court: The Untold Story of Thomas and George Boleyn* (London: I.B. Tauris, 2018), p. 263.
5. *Privy Purse Expenses of the Princess Mary, Daughter of King Henry the Eighth, Afterwards Queen Mary*, ed. by Frederick Madden (London: William Pickering, 1831), pp. 13, 17, 25, 51, 64, 65.
6. David Starkey, 'An Attendant Lord? Henry Parker, Lord Morley', in *'Triumphs of English': Henry Parker, Lord Morley, Translator to the Tudor Court: New Essays in Interpretation*, ed. by Marie Axton and James P. Carley (London: British Library, 2000), pp. 1–25 (p. 14).
7. Cal, SP. Span., V, ii. 21
8. 'Letter II: Sir William Kingston to Secretary Cromwell – On Queen Anne's Behaviour in Prison', in *The Life of Cardinal Wolsey*, by George Cavendish, Second Edition (London: Harding and Lepard, 1827), pp. 453-55 (pp. 453-54)
9. Diarmaid MacCulloch, *Thomas Cromwell: A Life* (London: Allen Lane, 2018), p. 347
10. Ibid.
11. George Wyatt, 'Extracts from the Life of Queen Anne Boleigne', in *The Life of Cardinal Wolsey*, by George Cavendish (London: Harding and Lepard, 1827), pp. 417-50 (p. 446)
12. Chelsea A. Reutcke, 'Martyr, Mother, Wife, and Queen: Anne Boleyn's Afterlife in the Shaping of the English Protestant Identity, 1558-c.1690' (unpublished Bachelor of Arts thesis, Wesleyan University, 2012), p. 57 <https://wesscholar. wesleyan.edu/cgi/viewcontent.cgi?article=1955&context=etd_hon_theses> [accessed 24 November 2018].
13. Ibid.

14. Ives, p. 194.
15. Ibid., p. 331.
16. Gilbert Burnet, *The History of the Reformation of the Church of England*, ed. by Nicholas Pocock (Oxford: Clarendon Press, 1865), I, p. 316.
17. Ibid.
18. '703a. John Husee to Lady Lisle, 24 May 1536', in *The Lisle Letters*, ed. by Muriel St. Clare Byrne, 6 vols (Chicago: University of Chicago Press, 1981), III, 377-78 (p. 378).
19. G. W. Bernard, *Anne Boleyn: Fatal Attractions* (New Haven: Yale University Press, 2011), p. 158.
20. Lancelot de Carles, *De Carles' Trial and Death of Queen Anne Boleyn: translated into Modern English*, trans. by Margaret Bolton (Berlin: Epubli, 2015), pp. 44-45.
21. Ives, p. 61.
22. de Carles, p. 44.
23. J. H. Baker, 'Spelman, Sir John (c. 1480-1546), Judge and Law Reporter', *Oxford Dictionary of National Biography* (Oxford University Press, 2008) <http://www.oxforddnb.com/view/10.1093/ref:odnb/9780198614128.001.0001/odnb-9780198614128-e-26105>
24. 'The Attainder of the Said Queen Anne', in *The Reports of Sir John Spelman*, ed. by J. H. Baker (London: Selden Society, 1977), I, 70-71 (p. 71).
25. LP, x. 908.
26. Paul Friedmann, *Anne Boleyn* (Gloucestershire: Amberley Publishing, 2013), p. 243; Ives, p. 191.
27. Fox, pp. 190-91.
28. Ibid., p. 191.
29. *Excerpta Historica, or, Illustrations of English History*, ed. by Samuel Bentley (London: Samuel Bentley, 1831), p. 262.
30. Ibid, p. 263.

Chapter 6: Aftermath of the Fall of the Boleyns

1. 'Letter CXXIV. Lady Rocheford to Secretary Cromwell', in *Original Letters, Illustrative of English History*, ed. by Henry Ellis, 3 vols (London: Harding, Triphook, and Lepard, 1825), II, 67-68.
2. LP, xi. 17.
3. George Cavendish, *The Life of Cardinal Wolsey*, ed. by Samuel Weller Singer (Chiswick: Harding, Triphook, and Lepard, 1825), II, p. 71.

Chapter 7: Serving the Third and Fourth Wives

1. *Privy Purse Expenses of the Princess Mary, Daughter of King Henry the Eighth, Afterwards Queen Mary*, ed. by Frederick Madden (London: William Pickering, 1831), p. 13.
2. 'Currency Converter', *The National Archives*, 2017 <http://www.nationalarchives.gov.uk/currency-converter/> [accessed 7 February 2019].
3. Charles Wriothesley, *A Chronicle of England during the Reign of the Tudors, from A.D. 1485 to 1559*, ed. by William Douglas Hamilton (Westminster: Camden Society, 1875), I, p. 64.
4. LP, xii. ii. 973.
5. LP, xii. ii. 1060.
6. Fox, p. 249.
7. Ibid., p. 250.
8. Ibid., p. 251-2
9. *Eccles. Mems.*, vol. 1, p. 2, pp. 462
10. Ibid.

Chapter 8: Confidante to Katherine Howard

1. Gareth Russell, *Young and Damned and Fair: The Life of Catherine Howard, Fifth Wife of King Henry VIII* (New York: Simon & Schuster, 2017), p. 16; Josephine Wilkinson, *Katherine Howard: The Tragic Story of Henry VIII's Fifth Queen* (London: John Murray, 2016), p. 6.

2. Retha M. Warnicke, 'Katherine [Catherine] [née Katherine Howard] (1518x24-1542)', *Oxford Dictionary of National Biography* (Oxford University Press, 2004).
3. Russell, p. 319.
4. Ibid., p. 198.
5. Ibid., f. 136.
6. SP 1/167 f. 133.
7. LP, xvi. 1134.
8. Ibid.; SP 1/167 f. 133.
9. Retha Warnicke, *Wicked Women of Tudor England: Queens, Aristocrats, Commoners,* Queenship and Power Series (New York: Palgrave Macmillan, 2012), p. 68.
10. David Starkey, *Six Wives: The Queens of Henry VIII* (London: Vintage, 2004), p. 675.
11. SP 1/167 f. 136.
12. Fox, p. 288.
13. LP, xvi. 712.
14. Russell, p. 199.
15. HMC Bath, II, p. 10.
16. LP, xvi. 832, 873, 905, 911.
17. SP 1/167 f. 131.
18. Ibid.
19. Ibid.
20. Russell, p. 229-30.
21. LP, xvi. 1338.
22. Ibid.
23. LP, xvi. 1339.

Chapter 9: The Downfall of Katherine Howard and Jane Parker

1. PPC, VII, p. 352-354.
2. Ibid., p. 352.
3. SP 1/167 f. 136.
4. HMC Bath, II, p. 9.

5. Fox, p. 298.

6. David Loades, *Catherine Howard: The Adulterous Wife of Henry VIII* (Gloucestershire: Amberley, 2014), p. 138.

7. SP 1/167 f. 131; Gareth Russell, *Young and Damned and Fair: The Life of Catherine Howard, Fifth Wife of King Henry VIII* (New York: Simon & Schuster, 2017), p. 230.

8. SP 1/167 f. 136.

9. Ibid.

10. Ibid.; HMC Bath, II, p. 9.

11. Cal, SP. Span., VI, i. 209.

12. Conor Byrne, *Katherine Howard: A New History* (Spain: MadeGlobal Publishing, 2014), p. 188.

13. Russell, p. 198.

14. Cal, SP. Span., VI, i. 209.

15. LP, xvi. 1340.

16. LP, xvii. 106.

Bibliography

Primary Sources

Manuscripts

British Library: *Cotton Manuscripts*, Vespasian F. XIII.
  Royal Manuscripts, 20. B. XXI.
Public Record Office: *State Papers, Foreign and Domestic, Henry VIII*, 1/167

Printed

Calendar of State Papers, Spain

Calendar of the Manuscripts of the Maqruis of Bath preserved at Longleat, Wiltshire

Cavendish, George, *The Life of Cardinal Wolsey*, ed. by Samuel Weller Singer (Chiswick: Harding, Triphook, and Lepard, 1825), II

Excerpta Historica, or, Illustrations of English History, ed. by Samuel Bentley (London: Samuel Bentley, 1831)

Hall, Edward, *Hall's Chronicle Containing the History of England, during the Reign of Henry the Fourth, and the Succeeding Monarchs, to the End of the Reign of Henry the Eighth* (London: J. Johnson, 1809)

Letters and Papers, Foreign and Domestic, Henry VIII

Original Letters, Illustrative of English History, ed. by Henry Ellis, 3 vols (London: Harding, Triphook, and Lepard, 1825)

Privy Purse Expenses of the Princess Mary, Daughter of King Henry the Eighth, Afterwards Queen Mary, ed. by Frederick Madden (London: William Pickering, 1831)

Proceedings and Ordinances of the Privy Council of England

Ecclesiastical Memorials Relating Chiefly to Religion and the Reformation of it, by John Strype, 3 vols (Oxford: Clarendon Press, 1820-1840)

The Chronicle of Calais in the Reigns of Henry VII and Henry VIII to

the Year 1540, ed. by John Gough Nicholas (London: Camden Society, 1846)

The Lisle Letters, ed. by Muriel St. Clare Byrne, 6 vols (Chicago: University of Chicago Press, 1981)

The Reports of Sir John Spelman, ed. by J. H. Baker (London: Selden Society, 1977),

Wriothesley, Charles, *A Chronicle of England during the Reign of the Tudors, from A.D. 1485 to 1559*, ed. by William Douglas Hamilton (Westminster: Camden Society, 1875), I

Secondary Sources

Burnet, Gilbert, *The History of the Reformation of the Church of England*, ed. by Nicholas Pocock (Oxford: Clarendon Press, 1865), I

Cherry, Clare, and Claire Ridgway, *George Boleyn: Tudor Poet, Courtier & Diplomat* (Spain: MadeGlobal Publishing, 2014)

'Currency Converter', *The National Archives*, 2017 <http://www. nationalarchives.gov.uk/currency-converter/> [accessed 7 February 2019]

Fox, Julia, *Jane Boleyn: The Infamous Lady Rochford* (London: Weidenfeld & Nicolson, 2008)

Friedmann, Paul, *Anne Boleyn* (Gloucestershire: Amberley Publishing, 2013)

Ives, Eric, *The Life and Death of Anne Boleyn* (Oxford: Blackwell, 2006)

Loades, David, *Catherine Howard: The Adulterous Wife of Henry VIII* (Gloucestershire: Amberley, 2014)

— — —, *The Boleyns: The Rise and Fall of a Tudor Family* (Gloucestershire: Amberley, 2011)

MacCulloch, Diarmaid, *Thomas Cromwell: A Life* (London: Allen Lane, 2018)

Mackay, Lauren, *Among the Wolves of Court: The Untold Story of Thomas and George Boleyn* (London: I.B. Tauris, 2018)

Russell, Gareth, *Young and Damned and Fair: The Life of Catherine*

Howard, Fifth Wife of King Henry VIII (New York: Simon & Schuster, 2017)

Somerset, Anne, *Ladies in Waiting: From the Tudors to the Present Day* (London: Phoenix, 2005)

Starkey, David, *Six Wives: The Queens of Henry VIII* (London: Vintage, 2004)

'Triumphs of English': Henry Parker, Lord Morley, Translator to the Tudor Court: New Essays in Interpretation, ed. by Marie Axton and James P. Carley (London: British Library, 2000)

Warnicke, Retha, 'Katherine [Catherine] [née Katherine Howard] (1518x24-1542)', *Oxford Dictionary of National Biography* (Oxford University Press, 2004)

— — —, *The Rise and Fall of Anne Boleyn: Family Politics at the Court of Henry VIII*, Canto (Cambridge: Cambridge University Press, 1993)

— — —, *Wicked Women of Tudor England: Queens, Aristocrats, Commoners*, Queenship and Power Series (New York: Palgrave Macmillan, 2012)

Wilkinson, Josephine, *Katherine Howard: The Tragic Story of Henry VIII's Fifth Queen* (London: John Murray, 2016)

Author Biography

Charlie Fenton is the author of the novel *Perseverance: A Novel of Anne Boleyn* and the non-fiction work *1066 and The Battle of Hastings in a Nutshell*. She has worked as the book reviewer for the Tudor Society since 2014 and runs the Facebook page and blog Through the Eyes of Anne Boleyn. She has recently completed an MA in Medieval and Early Modern Studies at the University of Kent in Canterbury and is embarking on a PhD on the effects of the Edwardian, Marian and Early Elizabeth regimes on the county of Kent.

Facebook pages: https://www.facebook.com/Through-the-Eyes-of-Anne-Boleyn-A-Research-Page-677356735641176/

https://www.facebook.com/Charlie-Fenton-950039418359182/

Twitter: @CharlieFenton2

Instagram: @charliefen

Recent bestsellers from Chronos Books are:

Lady Katherine Knollys
The Unacknowledged Daughter of King Henry VIII
Sarah-Beth Watkins
A comprehensive account of Katherine Knollys' questionable
paternity, her previously unexplored life in the Tudor court
and her intriguing relationship with Elizabeth I.
Paperback: 978-1-78279-585-8 ebook: 978-1-78279-584-1

Cromwell was Framed
Ireland 1649
Tom Reilly
Revealed: The definitive research that proves the Irish nation
owes Oliver Cromwell a huge posthumous apology for
wrongly convicting him of civilian atrocities in 1649.
Paperback: 978-1-78279-516-2 ebook: 978-1-78279-515-5

Why the CIA Killed JFK and Malcolm X
The Secret Drug Trade in Laos
John Koerner
A new groundbreaking work presenting evidence that the CIA
silenced JFK to protect its secret drug trade in Laos.
Paperback: 978-1-78279-701-2 ebook: 978-1-78279-700-5

The Disappearing Ninth Legion
A Popular History
Mark Olly
The Disappearing Ninth Legion examines hard evidence for the
foundation, development, mysterious disappearance, or possi-
ble continuation of Rome's lost Legion.
Paperback: 978-1-84694-559-5 ebook: 978-1-84694-931-9